Choosing Your Lawyer

An Insider's Practical Guide to Making a Really Good Choice

John Allison

John Allison

Published by The Coach for Lawyers, LLC
San Rafael, California
Printed in the United States of America

Preface

This book is written for people who are thinking about hiring a lawyer.

You may have never hired a lawyer before, or you may have a new legal matter that your current lawyer is unable to handle. You might simply be looking for some legal advice. Your business or non-profit group might need a lawyer to write a contract, to set up a retirement plan, or to represent the organization in a court case or regulatory proceeding. You might be thinking about starting a business or setting up a non-profit. You might be facing a personal legal matter such as a criminal charge, a bankruptcy, a civil lawsuit or a divorce. You might need a lawyer to make a claim or file a lawsuit on your behalf. Regardless of the reason you are thinking about hiring a lawyer, this book is written for you.

The first two chapters are introductory. They explain the consequences of the unique training lawyers receive and describe the intense competition and economic pressures within the legal profession that can affect you as a client. The remaining chapters will take you through a step-by-step process to identify lawyers with the skill and experience you need and then evaluate those lawyers before you decide which lawyer to hire. The quality of the experience you have with the lawyer you choose will depend more than anything else on how well you made the choice.

As a lawyer, I need to include a disclaimer: This book is not intended to give legal advice. My descriptions of the legal system and certain general legal principles may or may not apply to your situation in your jurisdiction. For legal advice I encourage you to ask the lawyer you choose!

John Allison   *August 2013*

Contents

1

Understanding Lawyers

Lawyers are people. Like all of us, lawyers have different personalities, skills, attitudes, knowledge and experiences. Some lawyers are friendly and reassuring while others are not. Some lawyers are good listeners, but many seem more interested in trying to impress other people with their technical knowledge and with stories about past victories. Most lawyers are discrete and protect their clients' confidential information very carefully, while a few like to boast about their skills at social functions and sometimes say too much. Many lawyers joined the profession to be of service to others, though some became lawyers to achieve social status and make a good deal of money. Most lawyers are trustworthy, but, sadly, a relatively small number are not. We can find people with these various qualities among the members of virtually any trade or profession.

What sets lawyers apart from the rest of us is their legal education and training. Nowadays, after obtaining a college degree nearly all lawyers spend at least three years in law school learning the law and learning how to think like a lawyer. Law students are taught how to apply statutes, regulations and case law to different factual situations, and how to distinguish one factual situation from another. This is a very logical, linear and rational process. Let's take a look at a couple of examples to see how the process works.

Suppose a state legislature wants to protect rivers from agricultural pollution, and passes a statute that provides: "Livestock shall not be pastured within 500 feet of any river."

Everyone understands that the statute would prevent a farmer in the state from allowing his herd of cows to graze along a river bank. But what if the farmer raises chickens and wants to build a chicken coop next to the river; are chickens "livestock" subject to the statute's prohibition? And what if a family owns riverfront property and wants to let their horse graze in the back yard; is a single horse considered to be "livestock?" And suppose a sheep ranch is located 100 feet away from a small creek that is dry for half the year; would the creek be considered to be a "river?" Lawyers love questions like these which create opportunities to make arguments about whether or not a law or regulation applies to a particular situation.

The way courts decide cases based on earlier precedents invites lawyers to analyze the precedents and make logical arguments about how they should be applied to the case being considered by the court. Since our culture values the rule of law, judges are reluctant to overturn or depart from a principle established in an earlier court case unless it is clearly out of date or contrary to evolving social policy. A classic example of the type of situation that can lead a court to overturn a precedent is the Supreme Court's 1954 decision in *Brown v. Board of Education*,[1] which overturned its 1896 decision in *Plessy v. Ferguson*[2] and established the principle that racially segregated schools are inherently unequal. The *Brown v. Board of Education* case illustrates the exceptional type of situation that can lead a court to overturn a precedent. Nearly all the time, judges consider themselves bound to follow earlier precedents that apply to the cases they are deciding, unless the precedents can be distinguished from the case being considered by the court. Lawyers in

---

[1] Brown v. Board of Education, 347 U.S. 483 (1954).
[2] Plessy v. Ferguson, 163 U.S. 537 (1896).

their role as advocates enjoy distinguishing precedents by crafting arguments to explain why the factual situation in their case is different from the facts in a precedent and why the precedent should not determine the outcome of their case.

These examples illustrate the logical, rational and linear thinking that is drilled into law students. They learn this way of thinking and problem solving in order to survive the law school experience and prepare themselves to take the bar examination they will need to pass in order to obtain a license to practice law. Law students practice this way of thinking over and over again, in their legal research and writing class, in preparing for and taking law school exams, in writing legal research memos and in moot court competitions. They graduate from law school having learned to "think like a lawyer."

So what's missing from the law school experience? Law students are not taught people skills. They are not taught about relationships among individuals or business associates. They are not taught about the challenges faced by a person who is trying to run a business. They are not really encouraged to be creative. Their focus is on learning and applying the law to a set of facts, rather than on problem solving and thinking "outside the box." They learn the adversarial process, where somebody wins and somebody else loses. They see the value of being highly competitive. They learn that a client's emotional experience of having a legal problem is simply not legally relevant. Their law school indoctrination has followed the view expressed centuries ago by Aristotle, "The law is reason free from passion."[3]

---

[3] See Bill Bradfield, ed., *The Book of Ancient Wisdom: Over 500 Inspiring Quotations from the Greeks* (Mineola, New York: Dover Publications, 2005): 61

After weeks of additional study, the law school graduates take a bar examination. Those who pass the exam become new lawyers. Today, most recent law school graduates become new lawyers before they have found a job in the legal profession.

2

The Legal Profession Today

The legal profession has changed dramatically over the years. Inspirational ideals of justice and service have been overshadowed by economic pressures and intense competition. Some lawyers have become cynical and disillusioned and only see clients as a means to an end. It is important to understand the current state of the legal profession so you can avoid the mistakes many clients make when they hire a lawyer.

The American Bar Association, which is the largest voluntary professional organization in the world, expresses lofty ideals for the legal profession. In the Preamble to its Model Rules of Professional Conduct the ABA states:[4]

> "[1] A lawyer, as a member of the legal
> profession, is a representative of clients,
> an officer of the legal system and a public
> citizen having special responsibility for
> the quality of justice."
>
> . . .
>
> "[6] As a public citizen, a lawyer
> should seek improvement of the law,
> access to the legal system, the
> administration of justice and the quality of

---

[4] Preamble, *ABA Model Rules of Professional Conduct* (2002).

service rendered by the legal profession.
As a member of a learned profession, a
lawyer should cultivate knowledge of the
law beyond its use for clients, employ
that knowledge in reform of the law
and work to strengthen legal education.
In addition, a lawyer should further
the public's understanding of and confidence
in the rule of law and the justice system
because legal institutions in a
constitutional democracy depend on
popular participation and support to
maintain their authority."

Many lawyers are inspired by these ideals. They chose the legal profession with a genuine desire to help other people. They may have made the choice wanting to be advocates for social change. They are committed to preserving and improving our system of justice. They want to do their part to make the world a better place.

As a whole, the legal profession takes the ethical rules governing lawyers very seriously. Most lawyers find it easy to follow the ethical rules because they are ethical people and act with integrity. They also honor and protect the attorney-client privilege which protects, with rare exceptions, the confidentiality of what a client tells his or her lawyer.

At the same time, the legal profession has become intensely competitive. Most law school graduates have a hard time finding jobs as lawyers and many are in debt with student loans. In many private law firms, lawyers are under constant pressure to increase their billings to clients and generate new business in order to keep their jobs and advance within the firm. Senior lawyers in those firms often feel they lack the time to mentor young lawyers and teach them the practical skills they need to practice law effectively. Law firms are under constant pressure to keep the clients they have and attract new clients. In recent years, a number of law firms have laid off lawyers or gone out of business. On top of these economic pressures, the lack of civility among lawyers seems to be at an all-time high. Professional journals and judicial opinions describe shocking examples of rudeness, name-calling, insults, threats and Rambo-style tactics by some lawyers who think that type of behavior will help their clients.[5]

These intense competitive and economic pressures, as well as the uncivil behavior by some lawyers, take their toll. In a 1999 law journal article entitled, "On Being a Happy, Healthy, and Ethical Member of an Unhappy, Unhealthy, and Unethical Profession," Patrick Schiltz, who was then a law school professor and is now a federal district court judge, reviewed studies about the mental and emotional health of lawyers and discussed the results of those studies.[6] When compared to the general population, lawyers are statistically more likely to be suffering from depression, psychological distress and alcoholism. While that is true, it is also important to remember that most lawyers are ethical. Despite the troubling statistics, most lawyers are as mentally

---

[5] For an in-depth discussion about the changes that have been taking place in the legal profession, see Anthony Kronman, *The Lost Lawyer: Failing Ideal of the Legal Profession* (Cambridge, Mass.: Harvard University Press, 1993) and Walter Bennett, *The Lawyer's Myth: Reviving Ideals in the Legal Profession* (Chicago: University of Chicago Press, 2001). Anthony Kronman is a law professor who served as Dean of Yale Law School. Walter Bennett practiced law as a trial lawyer and served as a trial court judge.
[6] Patrick J. Schiltz, "On Being a Happy, Healthy, and Ethical Member of an Unhappy, Unhealthy, and Unethical Profession," *Vanderbilt Law Review 52* (1999): 871.

and emotionally healthy and happy as the rest of us.

How can all of this affect you as a potential client? In several ways, making it important for you to learn as much as you can about a lawyer, and interview the lawyer, before deciding to hire him or her. A lawyer may be too stressed or too burned out to handle your legal matter well. A lawyer may be tempted to take on a matter for you that is outside the scope of the lawyer's skill and experience. A lawyer may take on a matter that the lawyer is really too busy to handle. A lawyer may drag out or overstaff a matter in order to generate more legal fees. A lawyer may suggest or promise a result that is overly optimistic, counting on his or her ability to explain away your disappointment later on by blaming the judge or blaming the jury if the case does not turn out well. Practical steps you can take to address these and other issues are discussed in the remaining chapters of this book.

3

Legal Skills and Experience

As you begin the process of choosing a lawyer, it is important to start by identifying lawyers who have skill and experience handling legal matters similar to yours. This is only the first step in the process. The other key steps and important factors to consider are discussed in chapters four through ten.

Only lawyers with skill and experience handling your type of legal matter should be considered. Otherwise, you run the risk of being represented by a lawyer who, no matter how well intentioned, may be learning how to handle your legal matter at your expense.

You may already have a solid professional relationship with a lawyer who has represented you well in the past. When that is the case, it makes sense to find out whether that lawyer has the necessary skill and experience to help you with your current legal matter. For example, the lawyer who worked on your estate plan may be able to write a contract for a real estate deal you are putting together. However, your estate plan lawyer may not have the skill and experience needed to represent you in a bankruptcy case, or to defend your son or daughter on a misdemeanor charge. As another example, the lawyer who represented your corporation in an employment discrimination case should be able to write an employee handbook for the company. However, that lawyer may not have the skill and experience needed to defend the corporation effectively in an environmental lawsuit.

If you need a new lawyer to handle your current legal matter, your candidates may be general practitioners or they may be specialists. Many general practitioners are excellent lawyers who are highly competent in several areas of the law. Specialists tend to limit their practice to specific areas, such as litigation, criminal defense, personal injury, patent law, bankruptcy or estate planning and probate, and they can be very effective as lawyers within their specialty. Regardless of whether you ultimately choose a general practitioner or a specialist, the first step in the process of choosing a lawyer is to understand your legal needs.

Established businesses and non-profits

If you are thinking about hiring a lawyer to represent your company or non-profit group, look for lawyers with skill and experience relevant to your organization's legal needs. For example, the organization may need one lawyer to prepare contracts and a different lawyer to handle patent and trademark issues. If you need a lawyer to represent your company or non-profit group in a court case, it is best to limit your search to lawyers who have proven their ability and willingness to take cases to trial. Lawyers with a reputation for being willing and able to take cases to trial will usually help you obtain a more favorable settlement in your case, and they will know how to try the case if it cannot be settled.

Setting up a business or a non-profit

You may be thinking about setting up a business or forming a non-profit organization. If that is the case, look for lawyers in your state who have experience setting up businesses or non-profits and who are at least generally familiar with the tax consequences of the various options that are available in your state. If you are setting up a for-profit business, your lawyer can help you decide whether to incorporate, whether to establish a partnership or form a limited liability company, how to structure the business organization you choose, and whether to make certain elections for income tax purposes.

Guidelines for personal legal matters

If you are looking for a lawyer to represent you or a family member in a personal legal matter, these guidelines should be helpful in identifying lawyers with the necessary legal skills and experience:

- To file for bankruptcy or obtain help with serious credit problems, limit your search to bankruptcy lawyers. Bankruptcy law and practice are highly specialized, and bankruptcy cases can only be filed in federal bankruptcy court.

- If you are facing or contemplating a divorce or marital dissolution, limit your search to lawyers who regularly handle divorce cases in the county where you and your spouse reside or the county where the divorce case has been or will be filed. The outcome of a divorce case can depend quite a bit on the county where it is filed. Since over ninety percent of cases are settled by agreement it is important for your lawyer to have strong negotiating skills. Your lawyer should also be familiar with the alternative dispute resolution processes that may be available depending on the level of conflict in your divorce, the impact on children and the potential for an amicable resolution.

The alternative dispute resolution process usually chosen is mediation, which is a facilitated negotiation. If you choose to participate in mediation your lawyer may participate directly or may simply advise and support you in working out agreements with your spouse. In many states there are family law lawyers who practice collaborative family law. The collaborative family law process, where it is available, makes it possible to resolve the case without going through an adversarial process in court, so long as both parties are willing to participate in the collaborative law process. In that process the parties agree their lawyers will represent them in negotiations and in preparing legal documents, but will not go to court on their behalf.

o   If you have been charged with driving under the influence (DUI), limit your search to lawyers who have experience defending DUI cases in the court where you have been charged. The defense of DUI cases is a specialized area and it is helpful to be represented by a lawyer who knows the judge and understands how the judge views DUI cases.

o   If you have been or may be charged with any other crime, limit your search to criminal defense lawyers, preferably ones who regularly practice in the court where you have been charged. It is helpful to be represented by an experienced criminal defense lawyer who knows the prosecutor and who knows the judge. Prosecutors have different attitudes about plea bargaining. Judges have different styles that may affect the way a criminal trial is conducted and they may have preconceived ideas about sentencing.

o Several other legal matters require a lawyer to have specialized knowledge and experience. These legal matters include worker's compensation claims, employment discrimination claims, workplace harassment claims, tax issues and tax liens, social security disability claims, estate planning, guardianships, immigration issues, export and import issues, patents, trademarks, water rights, oil and gas law and mineral rights. If you need legal assistance in any of these areas look for lawyers with significant relevant experience representing people in situations similar to yours.

o If you suffered a personal injury and want to make a claim against the responsible party or parties or against an insurance company, look for lawyers who have experience representing injured people and who are willing and able to take cases to trial. Most personal injury cases are resolved by settlement. An experienced injury lawyer who is willing and able to take a case to trial will be more effective in helping you obtain a fair settlement or a favorable verdict.

o If you are sued in a civil case, look for lawyers who have taken civil cases to trial. You will be in a better position to resolve the case on favorable terms if you are represented by an experienced civil trial lawyer who is willing and able to take a case to trial.

Special considerations for court cases

If you are hiring a lawyer for a civil or criminal court case, it is important to be represented by a lawyer who believes in you and your case. Your lawyer needs to be able to present, with credibility, the best possible case on your behalf based on the facts and the law. If your case will be tried by a jury, it is also important for your lawyer to be a good storyteller who can present your case in a way that has emotional appeal.

It can be helpful if your lawyer knows the judge and understands the demographics of the local jury pool. A lawyer who knows the judge will understand the judge's preferences for how a case is presented and argued and will also be aware of any preconceived ideas the judge might have about certain issues. Lawyers have different styles for presenting a case in court. Certain styles work well with some judges and not well with others. Some judges control proceedings in their courtroom very strictly, while others take a more relaxed approach and prefer to let the lawyers try their respective cases with minimal intervention by the judge. Some judges have attitudes about certain types of cases that may predispose them to rule in a particular way. It is important for your lawyer to understand these aspects of how the judge will preside over your case, whether it involves a personal legal matter or a dispute in which your company or other organization is involved. If the lawyer you ultimately choose does not know the judge, it will be a good idea for your lawyer to consult with a lawyer who does know the judge. The consultation will be well worth the relatively modest additional expense.

4

How to Find Lawyers

If you already have a professional relationship with a lawyer you like, it makes sense to first ask your lawyer whether he or she can personally handle your new legal matter. If your lawyer does not have the necessary skill and experience, your lawyer will probably refer you to another lawyer in the same law firm, though your lawyer might suggest a lawyer in a different firm. In either case, you should consider the recommended lawyer to be a possible candidate without feeling any obligation to hire that lawyer simply because your lawyer made the recommendation.

You can also receive recommendations from friends, relatives, colleagues at work, business associates or lawyers you know socially. You may want to consider the recommended lawyers as possible candidates, though it is very important to find out as much as you can about the basis for the recommendation. Did the person making the recommendation have personal experience with the lawyer? Did that experience involve a legal matter similar to yours, or were there significant differences? Did the person making the recommendation have needs, objectives and expectations that were different from yours? Was the person really happy with the lawyer? You should not feel any obligation to the referral source to hire a lawyer who was recommended. If a lawyer you know socially offers to handle your legal matter, you may want to consider that lawyer as a possible candidate. Just like any other candidate, it will be important to find out more information about the lawyer and interview the lawyer in a professional setting before making your choice.

You may have heard about a lawyer on the evening news or read about a lawyer in the newspaper. If the lawyer handles legal matters similar to yours and you like what you heard or read, you may want to consider that lawyer as a candidate.

Lawyer referral services provide information about lawyers who are willing to accept certain types of cases. Referral services are either sponsored or approved by a state or local bar association as a service to the public. They only identify lawyers and do not recommend or vouch for them. You can gain access to the lawyer referral service or services in your state online. The best way to start is to enter the name of your state bar association as the search term. For example, if you enter "iowa state bar association" a screen will come up that provides access to the lawyer referral service in Iowa (on that screen click "Find-A-Lawyer"). In other states it may take more than one step to gain access to the lawyer referral service. Illinois is an example. If you enter "illinois state bar association" the home page will come up. Click on "Public" and then on the next page click on "IllinoisLawyerFinder." On that page click on "Find A Lawyer." In some states, like California, you might be directed to a county bar association lawyer referral service or to other lawyer referral services that are approved, but not sponsored, by the state bar. Once you are on a lawyer referral service page, you can find lawyers by legal subject matter and geographic location. All of this can be done online.

A private referral source can be found online at www.martindale.com. Once you access that site, click on "I Want to: Find a lawyer or law firm." A form will appear, and you only need to enter the practice area, city and state and check the box "search for lawyers only." Click on "search" and a list of lawyers practicing in that field of law and geographic location will appear on the screen. The sponsor of this website is only providing information and is not recommending or vouching for the lawyers on the list.

You can also perform your own online search by entering the type of lawyer, city and state as the search term. For example, if you search "bankruptcy lawyer grand rapids mi" the search results will contain links to websites of bankruptcy lawyers practicing in Grand Rapids, Michigan.

You can also find lawyers in the yellow pages of the phone book under the category "Attorneys." They are listed in alphabetical order. At the end of the alphabetical list lawyers are often listed again by fields of law.

Finally, some lawyers pay for advertising in newspapers, on billboards, on television, on the Internet or in public places such as airports. You might want to consider lawyers who advertise their skill and experience representing clients in legal matters similar to yours. However, the only thing that sets those lawyers apart from others is that they paid money, perhaps a lot of money, to advertise. The fact that they paid for an advertisement does not mean they are better or more effective than other lawyers.

5

The Qualities to Look for in a Lawyer

The lawyers you have identified so far have the necessary legal skills and experience to handle your legal matter. Those lawyers can do the work. They know the law and they have represented other clients with legal matters similar to yours. What other qualities should you look for before you make your choice?

That question really has two parts. The first part of the question is general, and addresses the qualities and attributes some lawyers have that make them more effective as lawyers. Those qualities and attributes are not taught in law school. They are either part of a lawyer's nature or they have been learned from the lawyer's life experiences. The second part of the question is personal to you, and asks about a lawyer's personality, style and approach to resolving a legal matter that will put you at ease and make you feel good about being represented by that lawyer.

Building Trust

Qualities and behaviors that build trust are particularly important, because trust is at the heart of a successful professional relationship with a lawyer. You need to be able to have trust in your lawyer's judgment. You also need to feel comfortable sharing your deepest secrets with your lawyer. To be able to represent you effectively, your lawyer needs to know all the facts relating to your legal matter, including facts that are personally embarrassing or potentially harmful to your legal position. Your lawyer also needs to know what you want and how the legal matter is affecting you. With rare exceptions, the attorney-client privilege protects confidential communications between you and your lawyer. The attorney-client privilege exists so you can tell your lawyer everything relating to your legal matter and how you hope it will be resolved.

Here are some questions to ask yourself when you are considering whether to hire a specific lawyer:

o Does this lawyer's manner and demeanor inspire trust?

o Does this lawyer have good judgment?

o Is this lawyer a good listener?

o Does this lawyer want to understand my current legal situation and how I feel about it?

o Does this lawyer seem to care about how I would like my legal matter resolved?

o If I am looking for a lawyer to represent my company, does this lawyer want to understand my company's business?

o When I am meeting or talking on the phone with this lawyer, do I have the lawyer's undivided attention?

o Does this lawyer really care about helping me, or does this lawyer seem to have his or her own agenda?

o   Will I be able to trust this lawyer to give me the best possible advice for my situation even when it may not be the advice I am hoping to hear?

o   Will this lawyer keep my secrets?

Creative Problem Solving

Not all lawyers are good problem solvers. Too many lawyers identify the legal problem involved in a client's situation and then take a "checklist" approach to that legal problem. Having framed the client's situation as a legal problem, they simply go through the legal issues relating to the legal problem which they learned in law school and continuing legal education programs. Their law-focused approach, rather than a client-focused approach, prevents them from understanding the true nature of the problem to be solved, since legal issues are only part of a client's situation. Those lawyers are like doctors who prescribe aspirin for a headache without trying to figure out why the patient is having headaches. You will be much better served by a lawyer who is focused on finding the best way to address and help you resolve your situation. Three examples involving different areas of the law illustrate this point.

Suppose you have a boundary dispute with your next door neighbors. Though you've never really liked those neighbors and your relationship with them is strained, you know they have been planning to put their house on the market and move to a different state. They've been preparing their house for sale and just started building a fence on what you think is your side of the property line. You consult with a lawyer who takes the "checklist" approach and are told something like this: "If your neighbors are building a fence along what they have been treating as the property line, by planting trees, mowing the grass and generally using the land on their side of the fence line, and if they've been doing that openly and continuously for at least ten years, you might be out of luck. On the other hand, if you want me to represent you we'll need to start by having the property line surveyed. If the survey supports your position, I can send a nasty letter to your neighbors. If that doesn't work, we can take them to court."

Being less than completely satisfied, you decide to get a second opinion and are fortunate to consult with a lawyer who has good problem solving skills. That lawyer mentions that your neighbors' use of the disputed property for more than ten years could be an issue, but the most significant fact is that your neighbors will be putting their house on the market so they can move to another state. The last thing your neighbors want is for their property to be tied up in a lengthy court battle. This lawyer suggests: "Why don't you ask your neighbors if they would be willing to mediate this dispute and avoid a court case. You could each pay half the cost of hiring a neutral mediator. If a survey is needed, you might even agree to split the cost of an independent survey. The mediator can help you and your neighbors explore other concessions you both might make to resolve the boundary dispute without having to go to court. You could probably schedule a mediation session soon, before your neighbors put much more work into the fence and well before they're ready to put their house on the market." If your neighbors agree to mediation and the dispute is resolved, you will have avoided the hassle and considerable expense associated with a lawsuit. Your neighbors will be able to put their house on the market and, hopefully, sell it quickly and move away.

The next example involves a couple who immigrated as refugees from the former Soviet Union. They had been issued valid green cards and were lawfully residing in the United States for more than five years. They passed the examination to become naturalized citizens. After waiting a while to be notified about the date and place of their citizenship ceremony, they called the local U. S. Citizenship and Immigration Services (USCIS) office and were told to be patient. They waited longer and noticed that some friends who passed the citizenship exam after they had passed were already sworn in as citizens. They called USCIS again and were told, "Be patient. Don't call us. We'll call you when your ceremony is scheduled." After waiting a while longer, they contacted a lawyer and were told, "USCIS is performing a discretionary function and the court will not intervene; be patient." They continued to wait, and finally contacted a second lawyer who told them, "USCIS is performing a discretionary function and it's not smart to sue USCIS; keep waiting." Finally, they contacted a third lawyer who told them, "This isn't right. There has to be a remedy in court." That lawyer found a creative basis for a lawsuit, and filed suit against USCIS on their behalf. Since USCIS hadn't been sued before in a case like theirs, the agency did not have a procedure in place for dealing with the case. So what did USCIS do? They promptly settled the case by agreeing to the couple's citizenship petitions. The couple became citizens of the United States in a private swearing-in ceremony in the courtroom of a federal judge.

In the third example a woman was having medical problems and blamed the corporation that manufactured a product she was using. Based on extensive scientific research the manufacturer did not believe its product was causing her medical problems. The woman sued the manufacturer in a county court where, historically, out-of-state corporations seldom win. At a mediation of the lawsuit it became clear that an argument between the lawyers about what was causing the medical problems would go nowhere. The woman finally disclosed that all she really wanted was a one-story house so she wouldn't have to keep walking up and down stairs as she grew older. The lawsuit was settled when the manufacturer agreed to pay enough money for the woman to buy a modest one-story house and cover her closing costs and legal fees. She was relieved to look forward to having a suitable house for her twilight years. The manufacturer was glad to avoid the considerable expense and risk of taking the case to trial in a difficult and unfriendly jurisdiction.

These examples illustrate the benefits of finding a lawyer who looks for creative solutions to their clients' problems. To try to determine whether a lawyer will be an effective problem solver for you, notice the questions he or she asks. Is the lawyer really trying to understand what's at the core of your situation? Is the lawyer exploring alternative approaches to your legal matter and trying to figure out what would work best for you? Even though the lawyer has experience handling other clients' legal matters that are similar to yours, does the lawyer seem interested in finding out what is unique about your situation and how it affects you? When the lawyer describes his or her experience handling similar matters, do any of the examples indicate that the lawyer took a creative approach to resolving the client's problem? When the lawyer is discussing your situation with you and answering your questions, do you feel the lawyer is relating to you as a person rather than as a collection of legal issues?

Communications

Lawyers are assumed to be good communicators. After all, they talk and write for a living. However, many lawyers are not good listeners. Some lawyers have trouble explaining the risks of various alternative courses of action in a way that is meaningful to their clients. Lawyers can also have a hard time conveying bad news. The biggest complaint about lawyers as communicators is that they don't keep their clients well informed.

Here are some things to notice when you are meeting with a lawyer and trying to decide whether to hire that lawyer to represent you:

o   Do I understand what the lawyer is telling me?

o   Do I feel free to ask questions to clarify what the lawyer is telling me?

o   Do the lawyer's answers to my questions address my concerns?

o   Does the lawyer tell me what to expect as my legal matter progresses?

o   Can the lawyer give me an approximate timetable?

o   Is the lawyer willing to commit to keeping me informed in a timely way about progress and developments in my legal matter?

o   Do I feel the lawyer will tell me the truth about how my legal matter is progressing and will not try to "sugar coat" bad news?

o   Does the lawyer's communication style give me confidence that I will be represented effectively?

Reputation

A solid reputation is critical to a lawyer's effectiveness, especially if the lawyer is representing a client as an advocate. We really are known by the company we keep. A bad reputation will rub off on the lawyer's client. A good reputation will add credibility to the client's cause. People dealing with the lawyer who is representing you – such as the lawyer for the opposing party, the judge and other government officials – will assume that your lawyer's reputation is a reflection of you. They will make a similar assumption when a lawyer is representing your company or other organization.

A lawyer's reputation is a subjective quality based on what other people think. A good reputation is a solid foundation. Like the foundation for a structure, it is built with care over a period of time. Also like a structural foundation, a good reputation can be damaged or destroyed in an instant.

Ways to obtain information about a lawyer's reputation are discussed later in chapter eight. As you learn about a lawyer you are considering it will be helpful to develop a sense of what the answers to these questions are likely to be:

o Does the lawyer act with integrity?

o Is the lawyer honest?

o Do other people trust the lawyer?

o Can the lawyer be counted on to do what the lawyer promises to do?

o   Is the lawyer ethical, or does the lawyer tend to skate too close to the ethical line?

o   Is the lawyer knowledgeable and well prepared?

o   Does the lawyer treat other people with professional respect?

Rapport

Rapport is a personal quality that cannot be measured by any objective standard. It is the key to a successful professional relationship. Do you like the lawyer? Does the lawyer relate to you as a person and seem to understand you and your situation? Will you feel comfortable being represented by the lawyer? Only you can answer those questions.

Style

Lawyers have different styles, and their various styles appeal to different clients. It is important to find a lawyer whose style is consistent with the way you want your legal matter handled, regardless of whether the lawyer will be acting as your advisor or as your advocate.

If you are hiring a lawyer to act as your advocate, the lawyer's style is particularly important. As an advocate, the lawyer may be representing you in a negotiation, in a court case, in a regulatory proceeding or in dealings with a government official. Unlike some myths portrayed in movies and television programs, a lawyer can be highly effective as an advocate without being belligerent or nasty. A lawyer can be a very good negotiator without being contentious. Actually, a belligerent, nasty and contentious lawyer is likely to provoke a response from the opposing party that will make the legal matter more expensive for you and may even get in the way of a good outcome.

Consider this example. The owner of an established restaurant in a metropolitan area was approached by a developer who wanted to build a skyscraper. The developer already had architectural plans for the skyscraper and needed to buy the property where the restaurant was located. He was willing to have the restaurant rebuilt at a prime location on the main floor of the skyscraper. After some negotiations, the restaurant owner and the developer signed a contract which allowed the developer to buy the restaurant property and allowed the restaurant owner to rebuild the restaurant inside the skyscraper. After signing the contract the restaurant owner had second thoughts and went to see his lawyer. The lawyer wrote a nasty and contentious letter to the developer demanding a release from the contract. The developer's lawyer sent a blunt letter in response, basically saying, "Your client signed a contract, and if he's backing out we'll see you in court." After a number of sleepless nights, the restaurant owner called the developer and requested a meeting without their lawyers. The developer agreed, and when they met the restaurant owner explained that the restaurant had been a successful family business for several decades and the restaurant property was owned free and clear. He went on to say he'd been unable to sleep at night because he was in his early sixties and really didn't want to incur new debt to rebuild the restaurant. As a result of that meeting the developer changed the architectural plans to build the skyscraper around the restaurant property. The restaurant owner was able to keep the restaurant property and reclaim his peace of mind once he got his contentious and belligerent lawyer out of the way.

Effective advocates will make sure they fully understand their client's objectives and will stay focused on helping their client achieve those objectives. While they will thoroughly prepare their client's case for trial, they will also look for creative opportunities to resolve the case on favorable terms well before it reaches the courthouse steps. They will have strong negotiating skills to use when there is an opportunity to negotiate. They understand Abraham Lincoln's advice:

> "Discourage litigation. Persuade your neighbors to compromise whenever you can. Point out to them how the nominal winner is often a real loser – in fees, expenses, and waste of time."[7]

Effective advocates can be aggressive and firm when those skills are required, but they will not feel a need to prove how tough they are or how clever they are. They are comfortable with who they are. They have the inner strength and confidence to act professionally while representing their clients effectively.

---

[7] Abraham Lincoln, *Notes for a Law Lecture* (1850?).

6

Red Flags

Just as there are qualities to look for in a lawyer, there are also qualities and behaviors to avoid. Some red flags are fairly obvious. Others will become apparent as you learn about a lawyer from other people and from interviewing the lawyer. Ways you can discover red flags online are discussed in chapter eight. Evidence of a lawyer's red flags can be subtle. It is a good idea to trust your hunches and intuition.

Obvious red flags

Obvious red flags include slurred speech or the smell of alcohol on the lawyer's breath during business hours. You can find a skilled and experienced lawyer who is not impaired.

A lawyer who is rude or abusive towards his or her own staff will probably treat other people in a similar way. That type of behavior by your lawyer is likely to get in the way of the best possible resolution of your legal matter and may also cost you more money in legal fees.

Lawyers in financial difficulty

Lawyers, like anybody else, can be deeply in debt, can have tax liens against their assets, and can be having trouble making ends meet. Few lawyers actually steal from their clients, although that does happen. The more significant problem for a client is that a lawyer's financial difficulty may interfere with the lawyer's independent professional judgment on the client's behalf. If the lawyer is being paid by the hour, will the lawyer be tempted to find time to spend on work of marginal value in order to charge more legal fees? Will the lawyer drag the matter out in order to keep on billing? If the lawyer's fee will be a percentage of the money that is recovered for a client, will the lawyer encourage a settlement that sells the client short in order to receive the fee more quickly? As a client, you should not need to be asking yourself questions like these. Find a lawyer who is financially solid.

Lawyers pursuing their own agenda

A lawyer should be committed to handling your legal matter as effectively as possible on your behalf. You are entitled to the lawyer's best efforts and independent professional judgment, free of outside influences.

A lawyer may be interested in handling your matter as a means of proving a point the lawyer wants to make. During the representation, your interests in how the matter is resolved and the lawyer's desire to prove the point may diverge. If that happens, the lawyer's independent judgment will be compromised and you are likely to find yourself unable to continue to trust the lawyer. To be effective, lawyers need to be focused on their clients and their clients' interests, and not on themselves and their own agendas.

A lawyer may want to become a judge or may have other political ambitions that can get in the way of the lawyer's willingness to advocate your position as aggressively as needed to represent you effectively. A client needs a lawyer who is not afraid to "make waves."

While it is important for a lawyer to maintain professional

relationships with other lawyers and with judges, a lawyer should not put those relationships ahead of the client's interests. As an example, a lawyer once told a client, "I do not want to have to explain to the judge why I am going to take up the court's time to try a civil case that can be settled for $50,000." The client did not want to pay $50,000 to settle the case and was concerned that a settlement would only encourage other people to file similar lawsuits. The client had a very blunt conversation with the lawyer about the client's expectations and made it clear that the client was ready to find a different lawyer to take the case to trial. The lawyer backed down, went to trial and won the case. Later on, the client found a different lawyer to handle future legal matters because a client cannot feel comfortable being represented by a lawyer who seems to have divided loyalties.

Lawyers who seem eager to fight

Some lawyers are so caught up in the adversarial system that they seem eager for a fight, using terms to sell their services like "I'll fight for your rights" or "Let's teach that so-and-so a lesson!" or "Other lawyers think I'm Rambo." Hearing statements like that may have a certain amount of emotional appeal in the moment, but a lawyer who approaches an advocacy role with that mindset will pick unnecessary fights with the opposing party and may take extreme positions that are not helpful to the resolution of your case. A lawyer with that mindset will become so caught up in the battle that he or she will miss opportunities to resolve your legal matter well before it comes to trial and may lose objectivity in advising you whether or not to settle the case. Jury verdict reports across the country are full of examples of litigants who turned down reasonable settlement offers, presumably based on their lawyer's advice, only to lose their case completely at trial.

Lawyers who claim they never lose

There is a saying among experienced trial lawyers that, "A lawyer who never lost a case hasn't tried enough cases." If you are looking for a lawyer to represent you in a civil lawsuit, a contested divorce or a criminal case, be wary of lawyers who tell you they never lose even though they may be telling the truth. A skilled trial lawyer can make a big difference to the outcome of a case. However, judges and juries are unpredictable. Witnesses can do or say something unexpected when they testify. The court might schedule a case for trial just before the holidays, when jurors may become too impatient to fully absorb all the evidence. Most important, a case is allowed to go to trial because the judge has decided there is a genuine dispute between the parties. The most skillful trial lawyer in the country can lose a case simply because the opposing party had the better case.

The only way a lawyer can manage to never lose a case is to be very careful about which cases he or she is willing to take to trial. If you hire a lawyer who told you they never lost a case, don't be surprised if they change their tune shortly before trial and start telling you all the reasons why you should take the best settlement you can get. That happens because the lawyer is more interested in protecting an undefeated record than in helping you win the case. Maybe the case should be settled, but your settlement decision should be based on your lawyer's best independent professional advice, free of the lawyer's personal agenda.

If a lawyer tells you that he or she has never lost a case,

ask the lawyer three questions:

- o How many cases have you taken to a verdict or final judgment at trial?

- o Can you tell me about two of the most challenging cases you took to trial?

- o Would you be willing to take a case to trial that you might lose?

Unless you are really satisfied by the lawyer's answers to these questions, and by the lawyer's body language when answering the questions, find a different lawyer.

Lawyers who promise the moon

Do you remember the expression, "If it sounds too good to be true, it probably is?" For a number of reasons, the legal profession has become very competitive. The competition among lawyers for clients can be intense. Some lawyers make promises they cannot realistically keep in order to be hired by a client. If a lawyer suggests an outcome for your legal matter that seems too good to be true, at least get a second opinion from another lawyer before you decide which lawyer to hire.

This type of behavior comes up most often among some lawyers competing for clients who have been injured and want to make a claim for damages. Consider this example. Lawyer A tells a potential client, who was injured when a truck rear-ended the car she was driving, "I think I can get you $500,000." The client is disappointed, because she remembers being told by her best friend that lawyer B recovered a lot of money for her best friend's cousin. The client remembers enough about the cousin's accident to believe that her injuries are a lot more serious than the cousin's injuries were, so she makes an appointment with Lawyer B. At their meeting, Lawyer B tells her, "Your case is worth at least $2 million." She hires lawyer B, who files a lawsuit on her behalf. During the next six months, the client turns over her employment records, medical records, tax returns and other personal documents to the lawyer for the trucking company she sued. She also takes a day off work to give a deposition where she has to answer a number of personally embarrassing questions. The court then orders the parties to attend a settlement conference with one of the judges. The settlement judge tells the client that jury verdicts in cases similar to hers range between $400,000 and $500,000, and that she should consider herself lucky to get a $450,000 settlement. What had Lawyer B done? He promised the moon in order to be hired by the client, and was counting on a settlement judge to bring the client back down to earth. It is important to understand that Lawyer B had access to the jury verdict reports and should have known about local jury awards in similar cases. What does Lawyer B tell his client? He blames the settlement judge.

Ethical violations

The legal profession prides itself on being a self-policing profession. Each state has an office of professional responsibility or a lawyer's board that investigates ethical complaints against lawyers and makes disciplinary recommendations to the state supreme court or other licensing authority. Apart from situations involving a lawyer who mishandles client funds, disciplinary sanctions are relatively infrequent. This means that a lawyer who has been disciplined for an ethical violation will stand out from the crowd in a negative way. In most states, bar association journals and state bar websites publish reports of lawyer discipline. As a result, it is likely, at least in those states, that other lawyers and judges will be aware that a lawyer has been disciplined for an ethical violation. You will be better off with a different lawyer.

Marginal ethical behavior

Some lawyers have a reputation for skating too close to the ethical line by engaging in questionable behavior. They may have a reputation for dishonesty or stretching the truth, for failing to avoid conflicts of interest, or for acting in unprofessional ways. A lawyer with a reputation for marginal ethical behavior will not be trusted by other lawyers or by judges. You will be better off with a lawyer who is not carrying that baggage.

Too busy for you

Avoid lawyers who seem too busy to give your legal matter the personal attention you deserve, and lawyers who act as though your legal matter is not "important enough" for them. There are reasons why it might make sense for a lawyer to have a less senior lawyer or a paralegal work on some aspects of your legal matter. However, that should only happen with your approval. You are thinking about hiring a specific lawyer to handle your legal matter because of that lawyer's skill, experience and professional judgment. That lawyer needs to be personally committed to serving as your lawyer.

That uneasy feeling

In his book *Blink*,[8] Malcolm Gladwell explains how we subconsciously pick up subtle cues about a situation that we cannot explain because they do not rise to a level of awareness in our conscious mind. If there is something about a lawyer you are considering that makes you feel uncertain or uncomfortable, trust your instincts even if you cannot explain exactly what is bothering you.

Follow the red flags

No matter how much you might like a lawyer, or how much you might respect a person who recommended that lawyer, trust a red flag if you see one. Red flags will not simply go away. Remember what is at stake and how much money you will be spending on your legal matter. Find a different lawyer.

---

[8] Malcolm Gladwell, *Blink: The Power of Thinking Without Thinking* (New York: Little, Brown, 2005).

7

Legal Fees

Lawyers, generally speaking, have a well-earned reputation for being expensive. What might seem to be a fairly routine legal matter can cost several thousands of dollars. People have been known to spend well over a hundred thousand dollars to litigate a nasty divorce. Companies can spend millions of dollars to prosecute or defend complex litigation. Injured people might find themselves lucky to receive half of what their lawyer recovers from the responsible party or the insurance company, after legal fees and litigation costs are deducted from the total amount that is recovered.

To understand how much a lawyer is likely to charge you, it is very important to have a frank and specific discussion about legal fees with the lawyer. You are entitled to know how expensive the lawyer is likely to be, and how the legal fees will be calculated, before you decide to hire that lawyer.

There are three basic types of fee arrangements: a fixed fee, a contingent fee, and an hourly fee.

A fixed fee is a specified amount the lawyer will charge to perform the described service. As examples, many lawyers offer fixed fees to prepare a simple estate plan, to incorporate a small business, to file a patent application or to handle a simple bankruptcy. A fixed fee has the advantage of being predictable, as long as you and the lawyer have a clear understanding about what the fixed fee covers so you are not surprised with extra charges.

A contingent fee is usually based on a fraction or a

percentage of the amount of money the lawyer recovers for you. If the lawyer does not recover any money for you, then you will not have to pay a legal fee though you may be responsible for costs and expenses. The traditional contingent fee is one-third of the amount the lawyer recovers for you, although contingent fees of 40% are becoming more common in complex cases. Some contingent fee percentages are set by state law, such as the contingent fee that is allowed for handling worker's compensation claims. In class action cases, the contingent fee usually has to be approved by the judge. It is important to have a clear understanding with the lawyer about how the contingent fee will be calculated and how costs and expenses will be handled. To really understand how costs and expenses will be handed and to avoid an unpleasant surprise later on, ask these questions:

o   What costs and expenses will be taken out of the total amount that is recovered? Costs and expenses associated with handling a client's specific case usually include filing fees, process service fees, court reporter fees, expert witness fees, reasonable travel expenses and photocopy costs; will any other costs and expenses, such as a prorated portion of the lawyer's overhead costs, be taken out of the amount recovered?

o   Will costs and expenses be taken out of the total amount recovered before the lawyer's fee is calculated, or will they be taken out of your share of the recovery? If costs and expenses are taken out of your share, the lawyer will receive a larger fee and you will receive less money.

o Will you have to pay the lawyer for costs and expenses if nothing is recovered?

Fees based on hourly rates are the least predictable, unless you are able to negotiate a budget that the lawyer will not exceed without your prior approval. What hourly rates will you be charged? Will the lawyer raise those rates before your legal matter is resolved? If you ask how much the total fees, costs and expenses are likely to be, you may get a lawyer's favorite answer to just about any question: "It depends." Depends on what? An experienced lawyer should at least be able to give you an estimated range for each of the most likely scenarios. For example, if you are thinking about hiring a lawyer to represent you or your company in a civil lawsuit, the lawyer should be able to give you estimated ranges for total fees, costs and expenses for the first six months of the case, for litigating the case until a month or so before trial, and for taking the case to trial.

Recently, some lawyers have been willing to negotiate alternative fee arrangements that are really just a combination of one or more of the three basic types. For example, some lawyers may agree to a reduced hourly rate or a fixed fee that is coupled with an incentive bonus contingent on the outcome of the matter. Others may agree on a fixed fee for the initial phase of a legal project, with an hourly rate or a contingent fee if the legal matter proceeds past the initial phase. These examples are only illustrations. There are many types of alternative fee arrangements that some lawyers are willing to negotiate.

While legal fees are important and should be discussed candidly with the lawyers you are thinking about hiring, legal fees should not be the principal basis for your decision. Fees are only one of the many factors to consider. It is much more important make a really good overall choice in selecting the lawyer you hire than it is to choose what seems to be the "best deal" on legal fees.

Once you hire a lawyer, the way the lawyer's fee will be calculated as well as your responsibility for costs and expenses should be spelled out in a written agreement between you and the lawyer before the lawyer starts working on your legal matter. The agreement may be prepared as a formal retention and fee agreement or it may be contained in a letter.

8

How to Learn About Lawyers Online

There are four fairly easy steps you can take to learn quite a bit of information about specific lawyers if you have access to the Internet. It is important to take these steps so you will have as much information as possible about a lawyer before you interview the lawyer and before you decide whether to hire the lawyer.

The best way to start is by visiting the lawyer's website. Nearly all lawyers and law firms have websites. If you do not have a website address for the lawyer or the lawyer's firm, you can find the website by using the lawyer's name, the word lawyer and the lawyer's city as the search term. For example, if you are trying to find the website for John Doe in Denver, the search term would be: john doe lawyer denver. If John Doe or his law firm has a website, the search results will give you access to that website.

When you visit the website the home page will describe the firm and the firm's practice areas. Some law firms describe their practice areas very specifically. For example, firm A may be described as a litigation firm or a firm of courtroom lawyers, while firm B may be described as a firm that serves the needs of small businesses. Other firms may list the types of legal matters the lawyers in the firm handle. If a firm claims to be a "full service law firm" it is important to look closely at the firm's description of the types of legal matters its lawyers have actually handled. Other pages on the website will contain biographical information about the lawyer you are considering as well as information about the other lawyers in the firm. By navigating through the website you will develop a sense of the firm's culture and values and how the lawyer you are considering fits within the organization of the firm.

The next place to look for information is the Martindale-Hubbell® website which has profiles for many of the lawyers practicing in the United States. The website address is www.martindale.com. Once you access the site, click on "I Want to: Find a lawyer or law firm." In the form that appears, enter the lawyer's name, city and state. Click on "search" and the lawyer's name and contact information will appear, along with a list of the lawyer's practice areas and the lawyer's peer review rating. The lawyer's rating is the result of a peer review process established many years ago by the *Martindale-Hubbell® Law Directory*. Lawyers are surveyed periodically and asked to assess the ethical behavior and legal ability of their colleagues. Lawyers who are rated "very high" on the general ethical standards are eligible to receive a legal ability rating, which is based on a lawyer's legal knowledge, analytical capabilities, judgment, communication ability and legal experience. There are three Martindale-Hubbell® Peer Review Ratings™: AV Preeminent®, BV Distinguished® and Rated. All three ratings mean that the lawyer has been rated "very high" on the general ethical standards. An AV Preeminent® rating means that a lawyer's peers rank him or her at the highest levels of professional excellence. A BV Distinguished® rating is considered to be an excellent rating for a lawyer with some experience.[9]

The third source of information is the state bar association website for each of the states in which the lawyer is admitted to practice. You can find the website by entering the name of the state bar association as the search term. The home page should have one or more navigation tabs for information available to the public about lawyers in the state. In many states, that information will include information about whether a lawyer has been disciplined for an ethical violation. The navigation tabs will be different for the bar association websites in different states. For example, if you want to find out whether a lawyer admitted to practice in Virginia has been disciplined, enter the search term: virginia state bar association. On the home page, click on "Disciplined Attorneys" and then enter the name of the lawyer on the form that appears on the screen. As another example, if the lawyer is admitted to practice in the State of Washington enter the search term: washington state bar association. On the home page, click on "The Public" and then click on "Find a Lawyer" on the next screen. Enter the name of the lawyer on the form that appears and click on "Search." The lawyer's profile, including his or her disciplinary history, will appear on the screen. This is the most reliable way to find out whether a lawyer has been disciplined for an ethical violation if the bar association for the lawyer's state makes disciplinary information available to the public. It is important to note that state bar association websites do not disclose information about ethical complaints, pending disciplinary proceedings or private admonitions.

---

[9] More information about Martindale-Hubbell® Peer Review Ratings™ can be found at
http://www.martindale.com/products_and_services/peer_review_ratings.aspx.

The final step is to perform an Internet search about the specific lawyer you are considering, using the lawyer's name and city, and the word lawyer, as the search term: jane doe boston lawyer, for example. It is important to perform this search because the lawyer's website only contains information the lawyer wants the public to see, and state bar association websites do not report ethical violations unless a significant sanction has been imposed on the lawyer such as a formal reprimand or a suspension from the practice of law.

Your Internet search might reveal interesting and complimentary information about the lawyer, or it may reveal a red flag. Here are some red flags that were uncovered as the result of Internet searches performed in July 2013 about ten actual lawyers: *Lawyer A's* firm was disqualified as counsel in a case after the judge found that Lawyer A had lied about certain medical testing and had filed false claims. *Lawyer B* was sanctioned for refusing to dismiss a case that the judge had determined to be frivolous. *Lawyer C* was disqualified from a case when the judge found he had misrepresented important facts and breached a duty of care to his clients. *Lawyer D* was sanctioned for having improper contact with the judge about the merits of pending litigation. *Lawyer E* is facing discipline for filing pleadings in a court case that contained insulting language and slurs. *Lawyer F* was disqualified from continuing to represent a party in a lawsuit because he had previously represented the opposing party and obtained the opposing party's confidential information that was relevant to the lawsuit. *Lawyer G* had a financial interest in a company that sued a client of Lawyer G's law firm while Lawyer G had access to the law firm client's confidential information that was relevant to the lawsuit. *Lawyer H* was disqualified from continuing to represent a party in a lawsuit based on the lawyer's unprofessional conduct, which involved making demeaning comments about the opposing lawyer to the opposing lawyer's client and drawing lewd pictures while a witness was giving a deposition. *Lawyer I* was fined by a judge for improperly trying to withhold relevant financial documents from the opposing party during pretrial discovery. *Lawyer J* pled guilty to criminal charges involving campaign finance fraud.

A search performed in July 2013 of the bar association websites for the states where these ten lawyers are licensed to practice *only disclosed the discipline imposed on Lawyer J.* The search of the bar association websites did not indicate that Lawyer D and Lawyer E are facing discipline because pending disciplinary proceedings are not reported. Nothing was found in that search to indicate that formal ethical complaints have ever been filed against the other seven lawyers.

With the exception of Lawyer J, the only way to discover red flags like these is to perform an Internet search about each of the lawyers you are considering. That type of search will reveal information about a lawyer that is reported in news articles and professional journals which other lawyers and judges read. Lawyers also talk about other lawyers at bar association meetings and lawyers' social functions. This almost guarantees that other lawyers and judges where a lawyer practices will know about, or can easily learn about, the lawyer's red flags. You need to know about them as well.

9

The Interview

By this point you have identified one or more lawyers with skill and experience handling legal matters similar to yours. You may have decided to consider a lawyer recommended by your existing lawyer before looking for other candidates, or you may have several candidates on a list. You have learned as much as you can about each candidate from talking with other people and from performing your own research as described in the previous chapter. You may have eliminated some lawyers from further consideration based on red flags you already discovered.

The final step in the process of choosing a lawyer is to interview the lawyer. An interview is the only meaningful way to assess an individual lawyer's qualities and style and to see whether you and the lawyer have good rapport. It is best to interview a lawyer in person, if possible, so that you can see the lawyer's body language. Most communication between people is non-verbal, and body language cannot be seen in a telephone interview. A visit to a lawyer's office can also give you clues about the lawyer's personality, style and values.

Remember that the goal is to make a really good choice in selecting the lawyer who will handle your legal matter. You may decide to hire the first lawyer you interview. If you have more than one lawyer on a list of candidates when you start the interview process, it is a good idea to arrange the list in the order of your preference based on what you already know. Doing so will help shorten the interview process, since you do not need to keep interviewing lawyers once you have made your choice.

Most lawyers do not charge for an initial meeting with a potential client, which usually lasts for up to an hour. At the initial meeting you and the lawyer are really interviewing each other. The initial meeting will give you the chance to find the answers to these questions:

- o Does the lawyer really have the skill and experience to represent you well?

- o Does the lawyer have the qualities a lawyer needs to be effective?

- o Do you like the lawyer and will you feel comfortable having the lawyer represent you?

- o Will the lawyer be personally and actively involved in handling your legal matter?

- o Does the lawyer's style appeal to you and the way you want your legal matter handled?

- o Do you see any red flags?

- o Do you understand how the lawyer will charge you for legal fees and expenses, and approximately how much those charges are likely to be?

The lawyer will need to find out enough about your legal matter to make sure that representing you will not create a conflict of interest with an existing client or, in some cases, with a former client. A really good lawyer will also want to be satisfied that he or she is willing and able to help you. A lawyer who is not charging you for the initial meeting may give you general information about your legal matter and how it might be handled, but will probably not be willing to give you free legal advice.

When interviewing a lawyer it is important to be careful about how much information you disclose. What you tell a lawyer is not legally protected as privileged and confidential until an attorney-client relationship exists between you and the lawyer. An attorney-client relationship does not exist until you decide to hire the lawyer, the lawyer agrees to represent you, and you both reach an agreement on legal fees. A lawyer cannot agree to represent you until he or she makes sure that no ethical conflict exists that would preclude the representation. A conflict will exist if the lawyer or the lawyer's firm already represents a party adverse to you in a transaction or a dispute. A conflict may also exist if the lawyer or the lawyer's firm performed legal work in the past for a client who is now adverse to you.

The importance of being careful about disclosing information to a lawyer before an attorney-client relationship exists can be illustrated by two examples. Suppose you are thinking about buying a piece of commercial property to build an office park, and you are interviewing a lawyer with skill and experience handling real estate and property development matters. Before telling the lawyer the details of your plans, you need to make sure that the lawyer and the lawyer's firm do not already represent a client who might have interests adverse to yours, such as the owner of property you might want to buy, the property owner's real estate broker, or a property developer who is in competition with you. What you tell the lawyer in the initial interview will not be legally protected as privileged and confidential unless you hire that lawyer during the interview. As another example, suppose a bank employee is interviewing a criminal defense lawyer. It would be wise for the employee to describe his legal problem by saying something like this: "My bank is being audited by federal regulators and they may try to hold me responsible if there's a discrepancy in the financial reports." It would be unwise for the employee to blurt out: "I've embezzled over half a million dollars from the bank where I work and I think I'm about to get caught." What the bank employee tells the lawyer during the initial interview will not be legally protected as privileged and confidential until an attorney-client relationship exists between the bank employee and the lawyer.

You may want to consider setting up your interview as a consultation for the purpose of obtaining legal advice, so that an attorney-client relationship exists and the information you share with the lawyer will be legally protected as privileged and confidential. You will need to pay the lawyer a fee for the consultation. In a paid consultation, a lawyer will be willing to spend more time with you and give you at least preliminary advice about your legal matter. The lawyer may need to perform some initial research in order to give you a more complete legal opinion a little later. In any case, your time with the lawyer will give you the chance to decide whether or not to choose that lawyer to handle your legal matter. For this option to be available to you, the lawyer will need to be satisfied that an ethical conflict does not exist that would prevent the lawyer from representing you even on a limited basis. The lawyer will also need to be willing to accept a limited representation for a relatively modest fee, since even a limited representation might create an ethical conflict preventing the lawyer from representing someone else. If you decide to arrange for the initial interview as a paid consultation for the purpose of obtaining legal advice and the lawyer agrees, it will be important to make it clear that the lawyer is being hired only for the limited purpose of consulting with you and giving you advice about the best way to approach your legal matter. That will leave you free to choose a different lawyer to actually handle your legal matter, unless you decide that the lawyer you hired for the paid consultation is the one you want to choose.

10

Changing Lawyers

In an attorney-client relationship, as in any other relationship, there can be bumps in the road. You may find that the lawyer you chose is not as responsive as you had hoped or charges fees that seem too high. You may have concerns about the way your legal matter is progressing. You may not fully understand what your lawyer is doing on your behalf.

If you have any questions or concerns about your legal matter or the way it is being handled, you should discuss them with your lawyer. He or she should welcome the chance to answer your questions and address your concerns. If you feel your lawyer really listened to your concerns and made a good faith effort to address them, the professional relationship between you and your lawyer may actually be strengthened.

You should consider changing lawyers if you try to discuss your questions or concerns and your lawyer seems to be unavailable or defensive. If your lawyer listens to your concerns but you are not satisfied with the lawyer's response, it would be prudent to ask yourself whether you might have unreasonable expectations before you decide to change lawyers.

Changing lawyers may cost you more money in the long run, but having confidence in the lawyer who is representing you is very important for your peace of mind and for your lawyer's ability to represent you as effectively as possible. There is nothing wrong with changing lawyers. However, if you have hired a lawyer to represent you in a civil lawsuit or a contested divorce it is a good idea to try to avoid changing lawyers more than once. Clients who change lawyers two or more times in the same lawsuit or divorce case may undermine their own credibility. Judges and lawyers understand that the first lawyer a client hires may not work out for any number of reasons, but they start to wonder about clients who keep changing lawyers in the same lawsuit. They tend to think there may be something wrong with the client or with the client's case.

11

How You Can Tell that You Made a Really Good Choice

The lawyer you chose to represent you has been working on your legal matter for a while. You have been able to sleep well at night knowing that your legal matter is in capable hands. You trust your lawyer to do everything he or she can do on your behalf. You believe that your lawyer cares about your well being and is thinking about the best possible way to resolve your legal problem. You feel that your lawyer keeps you well informed. You are actively involved in your legal matter and feel comfortable raising any questions, concerns, doubts or fears with your lawyer, knowing they will be listened to and addressed. You understand the fees and expenses your lawyer is charging and believe they are reasonable under the circumstances. You would not hesitate to recommend your lawyer to your best friend, your closest relative or your business partner. If this describes the experience you are having with your lawyer, then you made a really good choice.

About the Author

John Allison has practiced law for 43 years. He built a successful private law practice as a trial lawyer and litigation attorney representing individuals, small businesses, non-profits and large companies. His law practice grew based on repeat business and referrals from satisfied clients. He also chaired a committee of the American Bar Association and served as a Judge *Pro Tem* in Seattle. After being in private practice for 24 years, John was hired by 3M Company to manage its litigation. At 3M he wrote the guidelines and criteria for hiring and evaluating lawyers in private practice. He hired and led teams of lawyers across the country representing 3M in high-profile cases.

More recently, John founded The Coach for Lawyers, LLC which is committed to expanding the capacity of the legal profession to respond to and serve the real needs of clients. The firm provides coaching for individual lawyers and law practice consulting services for law firms and legal departments.

John and his wife, Rebecca Picard, live in northern California. He can be contacted by sending an email to john@coachlawyers.com.